WILLOW
The Quantum Leap That Could Shatter Reality – ALL YOU NEED TO KNOW

How Google's Revolutionary Chip Is Reshaping AI, Computing, and the Future of Technology

J. Andy Peters

Table of Contents

Introduction

In a world where technology is evolving faster than ever, a groundbreaking development from Google has set the stage for a new era of computing. The announcement of *Willow*, Google's latest quantum chip, has left the tech world buzzing with excitement and speculation. For years, quantum computing has been a topic of fascination, a dream on the distant horizon. Now, Willow brings that dream closer to reality than anyone could have imagined, shattering the boundaries of what we thought possible in computing.

To understand why Willow is so revolutionary, it's important to grasp the basics of quantum computing. At its core, quantum computing challenges the very nature of how we process information. Traditional computers—your laptop, your phone, or even the most powerful supercomputers—rely on bits: tiny units of information that exist as either a 1 or a 0. These binary digits work in a linear fashion, performing calculations in a step-by-step manner. While this model has served us well, it has its limitations, especially when dealing with massive amounts of data or solving complex problems that would take traditional systems millennia to crack.

Quantum computers, on the other hand, use qubits—quantum bits—that operate under the strange principles of quantum physics. Unlike regular bits, qubits can exist in multiple states at once, thanks to two phenomena known as superposition and entanglement. This means that quantum computers don't just compute one solution at a time—they can process many possibilities simultaneously. It's like having multiple versions of yourself solving a problem at the same time, drastically speeding up computations.

What makes Willow so special is that it takes these fundamental quantum principles and applies them in a way that's both scalable and reliable. While many quantum computers in the past have struggled with maintaining stability as they grow more complex, Willow does the opposite. Instead of becoming more prone to errors as it scales, Willow actually becomes more efficient and reliable. This is a huge leap forward in the world of quantum computing, as it solves one of the biggest challenges faced by previous systems: error correction.

The significance of Google's breakthrough with Willow extends far beyond the world of computers. In the broader context of AI and technology, this chip has the potential to revolutionize entire industries. Artificial intelligence, which relies on vast amounts of data processing and machine learning, stands to gain immensely from the power of quantum computing. Problems that are currently too complex or time-consuming for traditional computers—whether in drug discovery, climate modeling, or cybersecurity—could soon be tackled at unprecedented speeds. Willow doesn't just represent an incremental step forward in technology; it's the dawn of a new quantum era, one that could reshape the very fabric of the digital world as we know it.

Google's announcement is a sign of things to come. Quantum computing is no longer a distant dream; it's becoming a reality that will drive innovation in ways we're only beginning to understand. As we explore the breakthroughs behind Willow, we'll uncover the incredible potential this quantum leap holds for the future of technology, AI, and beyond.

Chapter 1: Understanding Quantum Computing and Its Power

At its core, quantum computing is an entirely new way of processing information, one that challenges everything we know about traditional computing. To understand how quantum computing works, it helps to first explore some of the basics of quantum physics, the field of science that underpins this revolutionary technology.

Quantum physics, at its heart, deals with the behavior of matter and energy on the smallest scales—on the scale of atoms and subatomic particles. In this strange realm, particles don't behave in ways we're accustomed to seeing in the everyday world. Instead of following predictable paths, they behave probabilistically, meaning they can exist in multiple states at once, and their interactions are deeply interconnected in ways that classical physics can't explain.

It's this weirdness of the quantum world that quantum computers exploit. Whereas classical computers rely on a predictable, linear processing of data, quantum computers use the principles of quantum mechanics to perform calculations in ways that classical systems simply cannot.

Before diving into quantum computing, it's essential to understand how traditional, or "classical," computers work. These systems process information using **bits**—the smallest unit of data. A bit is binary, meaning it can only exist in one of two states: a 1 or a 0. These bits are the foundation of every operation that a classical computer performs, from basic arithmetic to running complex algorithms.

Classical computers process tasks step by step, turning individual bits into larger structures of data. Whether you're using a phone, a laptop, or a supercomputer, they all follow this fundamental approach. While traditional computers have become incredibly fast and efficient, they still face significant limitations, particularly when tasked with solving extremely complex problems like simulating molecules or analyzing enormous datasets.

Quantum computing, on the other hand, uses **qubits** (quantum bits) instead of regular bits. While bits are confined to a single state (either 0 or 1), qubits have the unique ability to exist in a state of **superposition**. This means they can be both 0 and 1 at the same time, or anywhere in between, until they are measured. Imagine being able to explore all possible paths of a decision simultaneously, instead of having to go down one path at a time. This ability to represent multiple possibilities at once gives quantum computers a massive parallel processing advantage over classical systems.

But that's not all. Quantum computers can also harness the power of **entanglement**, a phenomenon where qubits become linked in such a way that the state of one qubit can instantaneously affect the state of another, no matter how far apart they are. This interconnectedness allows quantum computers to share information between qubits in ways that classical systems cannot replicate. In a quantum computer, this entanglement leads to a more powerful and efficient exchange of information, making it possible to perform computations far beyond the reach of classical systems.

The third key concept that quantum computers rely on is **interference**. In quantum mechanics, particles can interfere with one another, either reinforcing or canceling each other out. In the world of quantum computing, this property allows the computer to enhance the probability of correct answers while diminishing the chances of errors.

When qubits perform calculations, they don't just generate random results. They interfere with one another in a way that guides them toward the most likely solution. This makes quantum computers incredibly efficient when solving certain types of problems, particularly those that involve large amounts of data or require exploring many possibilities at once.

In classical computing, the process of running through possibilities is linear and often involves trying different approaches sequentially. With quantum computing, however, multiple solutions are tested simultaneously, and the correct one is reinforced by quantum interference, making the process exponentially faster and more efficient.

Quantum computing harnesses the power of superposition, entanglement, and interference to solve problems in a radically different way than classical computers. While classical systems can only explore one possibility at a time, quantum computers can explore countless possibilities in parallel, giving them the ability to tackle problems that would take classical systems millions of years to solve.

In essence, quantum computing is not just an incremental improvement over classical computing; it represents a fundamental shift in how we think about computation itself. By using the strange and powerful principles of quantum mechanics, quantum computers can solve problems that were once thought to be beyond the reach of any computer, no matter how powerful. This breakthrough promises to unlock new frontiers in artificial intelligence, medicine, energy, and beyond, revolutionizing industries and shaping the future of technology.

Quantum computers are not merely faster versions of traditional computers; they operate under an entirely different set of rules, thanks to the strange and powerful principles of quantum mechanics. While classical computers are limited by their binary nature—processing information in a series of 0s and 1s—quantum computers harness the bizarre properties of quantum physics to perform computations in ways that were once thought impossible. These unique characteristics give quantum computers an immense power difference over their traditional counterparts, allowing them to solve complex problems far beyond the reach of even the most advanced classical machines.

One of the key features that make quantum computers so different is their ability to leverage **superposition**, which allows qubits to exist in multiple states at once. This means that a quantum computer can process many different possibilities simultaneously, whereas a traditional computer would need to work through each possibility one by one. When combined with **entanglement**, the phenomenon where qubits become linked and influence each other instantaneously, quantum computers can perform parallel computations that classical systems simply cannot. Entanglement enables faster processing of information, and when paired with quantum **interference**, the results can be amplified and directed toward the correct answer, drastically improving efficiency.

The power difference between traditional computers and quantum computers is nothing short of staggering. Take, for example, the challenge of factoring large numbers—an essential task in cryptography. Classical computers use algorithms that are efficient for small numbers but become exponentially slower as the numbers grow larger. A quantum computer, however, could use **Shor's algorithm**, which takes advantage of quantum entanglement and superposition, to factor numbers exponentially faster than any classical algorithm could. This capability would render many current encryption systems, which rely on the difficulty of large number factorization, vulnerable to attack by quantum computers.

The potential real-world applications of quantum computing are equally revolutionary. In the field of **artificial intelligence (AI)**, quantum computers could dramatically speed up machine learning algorithms, enabling them to process and analyze vast datasets in ways that are impossible for classical systems. Quantum-enhanced AI could lead to breakthroughs in areas like pattern recognition, natural language processing, and decision-making.

In **cryptography**, quantum computing could not only break existing encryption methods but also pave the way for more secure forms of encryption through quantum key distribution. By leveraging the principles of quantum mechanics, future quantum encryption techniques could make data transmission virtually unhackable, offering unprecedented levels of security.

In the **pharmaceutical industry**, quantum computers hold the potential to revolutionize drug discovery. Simulating molecular structures and chemical reactions is a complex and time-consuming process for classical computers, but quantum systems could perform these simulations far more efficiently. By understanding molecular behavior at a quantum level, researchers could discover new drugs and treatments faster than ever before, opening up new frontiers in medicine.

The possibilities seem limitless. As quantum computing technology advances, it will inevitably reshape a wide array of industries, enabling us to solve problems that were once thought unsolvable and opening the door to innovations that could transform our world in ways we can't yet fully imagine. The race to unlock the full potential of quantum computers is only just beginning, but the impact they will have on fields ranging from medicine to security to AI will likely be felt for generations to come.

Chapter 2: The Evolution of Google's Quantum Journey

Google's journey into the world of quantum computing has been both groundbreaking and ambitious. It all started with the company's desire to push the boundaries of computation, not just in terms of speed but also in fundamentally reshaping how we think about computing itself. Quantum computing was a bold leap into the unknown—a way of harnessing the oddities of quantum mechanics to solve problems that were previously deemed impossible for classical computers.

Before Willow, Google made its first major mark on the quantum computing landscape with **Sycamore**, a quantum processor that made headlines in 2019 for achieving **quantum supremacy**—a term that refers to the point at which a quantum computer can perform a calculation that would be practically impossible for the most powerful classical supercomputers. Sycamore was able to solve a highly specialized problem in 200 seconds, a task that would have taken the world's fastest supercomputer over 10,000 years. This milestone was a monumental achievement, signaling that quantum computing wasn't just a theoretical pursuit but a tangible reality with the potential to revolutionize entire industries.

But despite the success of Sycamore, quantum computing was still in its infancy. Sycamore's feat was impressive, but it was limited in scope and could only perform a very specific task. Google's team, however, was not satisfied with just proving that quantum computing could work. They set their sights on overcoming the challenges that still plagued the field, such as error rates, scalability, and the fragility of qubits.

This is where **Willow** comes into play. Unlike Sycamore, Willow isn't just another demonstration of quantum computing in action—it's the culmination of years of research, innovation, and hard-won breakthroughs. While Sycamore was an important stepping stone, Willow addresses some of the critical issues that have plagued quantum computing, such as its vulnerability to errors and its inability to scale effectively.

One of the standout features of Willow is its ability to **self-correct**. Unlike Sycamore and other quantum processors that struggle with the errors introduced by qubits, Willow's design allows it to get better at fixing these errors as it scales up. This is a fundamental breakthrough. Traditionally, as quantum computers increase in size, their error rates grow, leading to unreliable results. But Willow flips this paradigm. By making its quantum systems more robust, Willow manages to reduce the number of errors even as the system gets larger, making it not just powerful but highly reliable.

Another aspect that makes Willow stand out is its **scalability**. Previous quantum processors, like Sycamore, could only handle a limited number of qubits. But Willow pushes the envelope, showing that as the number of qubits increases, the system becomes even more stable. This is a crucial step in quantum computing because scalability is essential for quantum computers to tackle real-world problems in industries like pharmaceuticals, cryptography, and artificial intelligence. Willow's ability to maintain its quantum properties even as it grows in size is a game-changer, one that paves the way for more practical and widespread applications.

Google's vision for Willow is clear: to build a quantum computer that not only works but works reliably and at scale. With Willow, Google has created a quantum system that brings us closer to harnessing the true potential of quantum mechanics for real-world applications, while addressing the critical issues that have held back earlier attempts in the field. It's not just a quantum computer; it's a leap toward the future of technology. Willow stands as a symbol of what is possible when innovation, determination, and vision come together in the pursuit of something truly transformative.

Willow is more than just another quantum processor—it's a leap forward in the evolution of quantum computing. Google's relentless pursuit of a truly scalable and reliable quantum computer has culminated in a design that addresses many of the challenges that have plagued quantum technology for years. Where previous quantum processors like Sycamore showcased the potential of quantum computing, Willow goes further by making these capabilities more practical, robust, and ready for real-world applications.

One of the most remarkable features of Willow is its ability to **handle errors** in ways that were previously thought impossible. In traditional quantum computing, error correction is a monumental challenge. The delicate nature of qubits—the fundamental units of quantum information—means that they are highly susceptible to interference from their environment.

This leads to **quantum decoherence**, where the information stored in qubits becomes corrupted, resulting in incorrect calculations. As quantum systems increase in size, this issue only becomes more pronounced. In many previous attempts, scaling up the number of qubits meant increasing the likelihood of errors, making large-scale quantum computations impractical.

But Willow has flipped this problem on its head. Instead of the error rate increasing as the number of qubits grows, Willow's design incorporates a powerful **error correction mechanism** that actually improves as the system scales. Google's team achieved this breakthrough by leveraging a technique known as **quantum error correction codes**, which allows the quantum processor to detect and correct errors on the fly. This makes Willow not only more reliable but also far more efficient at solving complex problems that traditional quantum processors couldn't handle.

The real magic of Willow lies in its **105 qubits**. While this may not seem like a huge number compared to some classical computers, it's a massive achievement in the quantum world. Most previous quantum processors operated with fewer qubits, and as the number of qubits increased, the system became more prone to errors. Willow's ability to scale up to 105 qubits while maintaining a high degree of reliability is a testament to the sophistication of its design. Each qubit in Willow is highly entangled with others, creating a vast network of quantum connections that allows for incredibly complex computations to occur in parallel.

What sets Willow apart from other quantum processors is the way it uses these 105 qubits. Rather than simply stacking more qubits to increase computational power, Willow leverages the **interconnectedness of qubits** in a way that amplifies its error-correcting abilities. With the addition of each new qubit, the system doesn't just increase in raw processing power—it becomes more stable and accurate. This is a direct result of Willow's novel design, which encourages qubits to collaborate and self-correct as part of a larger, interconnected network. It's a game-changing approach that makes Willow far more reliable than previous quantum processors.

Additionally, Willow's advancements in **error correction** don't just apply to its 105 qubits. Google has demonstrated that Willow can handle a far more complex error correction scheme than anything that has been achieved before. In simple terms, the more qubits you add to a quantum processor, the more opportunities there are for errors. But Willow proves that adding more qubits doesn't have to come at the expense of accuracy or performance. Instead, it makes each qubit work harder to catch and correct errors, ensuring that the system as a whole is more reliable and less prone to failure.

This combination of scaling qubits, maintaining coherence, and ensuring error correction has set Willow apart from its predecessors. Google has managed to take the fragile nature of quantum information and turn it into a strength, creating a system that is capable of solving problems that were once thought to be beyond the reach of even the most powerful computers. Willow is a bold step toward the future, where quantum systems are not just powerful but also resilient and ready to tackle the most complex challenges in fields like artificial intelligence, cryptography, and drug discovery.

In short, Willow isn't just a quantum processor—it's a whole new way of thinking about what quantum computers can achieve. By overcoming the long-standing obstacles of error correction and scalability, Willow has set the stage for a new era in computing, where the most complex problems can be solved in ways we once thought impossible.

Chapter 3: The Game-Changing Technology

Willow's most significant achievement lies in its ability to **defy classical limits** in the realm of quantum computing. For years, the idea that quantum systems could scale effectively without succumbing to errors was nothing more than a distant dream. This issue has been the Achilles' heel of quantum computing, with each attempt to increase the number of qubits in a system usually leading to greater errors, making large quantum systems virtually unusable. But with Willow, Google has fundamentally redefined the rules of what is possible in quantum computation. Instead of becoming more error-prone as it grows, Willow gets **better** at correcting its mistakes as the system scales up.

In classical computing, the basic unit of information is the **bit**, which can be either a 0 or a 1. These bits are processed and manipulated according to the rules of classical logic. But quantum computing operates on a completely different set of principles, thanks to the unique properties of **qubits**—the quantum equivalent of bits. The power of quantum computing comes from the fact that qubits can exist in multiple states at once, thanks to quantum phenomena like **superposition** and **entanglement**. These properties allow quantum computers to perform many calculations simultaneously, which leads to an immense potential for speed and power.

However, as quantum systems get larger, the challenge of error correction becomes exponentially more difficult. The more qubits there are, the more susceptible the system is to interference, leading to corrupted data. In traditional quantum computers, this problem has been so severe that scaling up often resulted in more errors than the system could handle. **Error correction** in classical systems is relatively straightforward—additional redundancy can be added to ensure that errors are detected and fixed. But quantum error correction has been a different beast entirely. Quantum information is delicate, and the very act of measuring or observing qubits can alter their state, leading to more errors. This is why traditional methods of error correction don't work in quantum systems.

Willow breaks this pattern with a revolutionary **error-correction system**. As the number of qubits increases, Willow's error-correction capabilities improve rather than degrade. To understand why this is so remarkable, imagine a growing team of workers tasked with solving a series of problems. In a traditional system, as the team grows, the likelihood of mistakes increases because the workers start to become overwhelmed by the complexity of the task. But with Willow, the opposite happens: as the team grows, the workers are able to **fix more mistakes simultaneously**, becoming more effective at catching and correcting errors as they arise.

To visualize this, think of a grid of workers, each assigned to a task of checking for errors. In a small team, say a 3x3 grid, each worker can only correct one mistake at a time. It's basic and functional but limited. Now imagine scaling up to a 5x5 grid, where the team expands to 49 workers. This larger team can now handle **two mistakes at once**, showing that as the team gets bigger, it becomes more efficient at error correction. Now, let's scale up even further to a 7x7 grid, with 97 workers. At this level, the team can handle **three mistakes simultaneously**, and the system continues to improve as it grows. The larger the grid, the more mistakes it can handle at once—without getting bogged down by the added complexity.

This analogy perfectly captures the essence of Willow's **error-correction system**. In a traditional quantum system, increasing the number of qubits leads to more mistakes, making error correction harder. But Willow takes the opposite approach: by making the system larger and more complex, it **becomes better at self-correcting**. The added qubits act like extra workers in the team, each one capable of checking the others' work and ensuring the system as a whole runs smoothly. Instead of chaos, Willow turns size into an asset.

The breakthrough with Willow's design lies in the way these qubits work together to catch and correct errors. The **connections** between them—represented by the yellow links in the grid analogy—serve as a **safety net** that strengthens as the system grows. This network of interlinked qubits ensures that when one qubit starts to show signs of error, the other qubits can work together to restore the integrity of the entire system. The end result is a quantum processor that **scales up effectively**, not by simply adding more processing power, but by improving its **resilience and reliability** as it grows. This is the critical distinction that sets Willow apart from its predecessors.

What makes this even more impressive is that Willow isn't just better at handling errors in small-scale systems. Google's team has demonstrated that the more qubits Willow has, the more reliably it operates, making it a quantum system that can tackle ever-more complex problems without losing its edge. This breakthrough is crucial for the future of quantum computing, as it paves the way for larger, more powerful quantum systems that can handle tasks beyond the capabilities of classical computers.

Willow is rewriting the story of quantum error correction, showing that it's not just possible to build larger quantum systems, but that those systems can **work better** as they scale. This ability to improve error correction as the system grows could be the key to unlocking the full potential of quantum computing and making it a reliable, everyday tool for solving problems in AI, cryptography, pharmaceuticals, and beyond. With Willow, Google has proven that **bigger can be better**—and that the road to truly scalable quantum computing is within reach.

Willow's revolutionary approach to handling errors is what truly sets it apart in the world of quantum computing. Traditionally, the concept of **error correction** in quantum systems has been one of the biggest challenges. As quantum systems scale up, adding more qubits often leads to more errors rather than fewer. The nature of quantum mechanics makes error correction complex—because qubits are fragile, their states are easily disturbed by interference or external factors. In older quantum systems, this caused chaos, with additional qubits amplifying the problem instead of solving it. More qubits led to more mistakes, and instead of improving the system, the errors grew exponentially, crippling the performance of the quantum processor.

But with Willow, Google has fundamentally reimagined how quantum systems can handle errors. Instead of falling victim to the conventional pitfalls of scaling, Willow's design is built on the principle that **more qubits** do not mean more errors; in fact, they mean fewer. Willow's innovation lies in its **self-correcting quantum**

system, a mechanism that gets more efficient as the system grows. While traditional systems struggled with the increasing complexity of error correction as the number of qubits increased, Willow turns that idea on its head. In this new paradigm, adding more qubits actually **improves** the system's reliability, making it more adept at identifying and correcting errors before they cause significant problems.

To understand how this works, imagine a grid of workers tasked with fixing mistakes in a process. In a traditional quantum system, as you add more workers, the process becomes more chaotic because the workers are overwhelmed by the complexity of the system, and mistakes multiply. However, Willow's system functions like a well-organized team, where each new worker is an asset, contributing to a **more efficient** error-correction process. Rather than becoming overwhelmed, the team grows stronger and more capable as more workers are added.

Visualizing this process is easiest by imagining different grid sizes. Picture a small grid of 3x3, with just nine workers. This team is relatively simple and can only handle a limited number of mistakes at once. The small team is functional but far from ideal. Now, imagine expanding the grid to 5x5. With 25 workers, the team can now handle more mistakes simultaneously. The larger grid allows for greater coordination among the workers, and their ability to detect and correct errors improves significantly. But what happens when the team is expanded even further to a 7x7 grid with 49 workers? At this stage, the system becomes incredibly efficient, handling multiple errors simultaneously and becoming far more resilient to failure.

In Willow's case, this scaling up is not just about quantity—it's about **quality**. As the quantum processor grows, the error-correction capabilities grow with it. Each added qubit strengthens the system's ability to detect errors, enabling it to handle even the most complex computations without falling victim to the kinds of mistakes that traditionally plague larger quantum systems. This **self-correcting mechanism** means that the quantum system becomes **more stable as it grows**, rather than becoming more unstable like in traditional systems.

To put this into context, let's think of Willow's error-correction process in terms of a traffic system. In a traditional system, the more cars you add to the roads, the more traffic jams you get. The system becomes congested, and the cars struggle to move efficiently. But with Willow, it's as if each new car is not just an additional vehicle, but a **traffic officer** that helps direct and manage the flow. The more cars there are, the smoother the traffic becomes. The addition of more qubits in Willow's system results in a **greater capacity to self-manage** errors, much like the cars (or workers) learning to coordinate better as more are added.

This self-correcting feature of Willow is essential for its ability to scale up and handle far more complex problems than any previous quantum system. By using a system of interlinked qubits, Willow can detect and correct errors in real time, minimizing the risk of data corruption. As the quantum processor continues to grow, Willow's error-correction mechanisms improve, ensuring that the system remains stable and accurate no matter how large or complex the task at hand.

In practical terms, this innovation could have far-reaching implications for industries that rely on large-scale quantum computations, such as **pharmaceuticals**, **cryptography**, and **artificial intelligence**. By ensuring that quantum systems can scale effectively without compromising accuracy or reliability, Willow opens the door to tackling real-world problems that classical computers could never dream of solving. From breaking the codes of complex genetic sequences to simulating the behaviors of molecules for drug discovery, Willow's ability to self-correct as it scales could revolutionize the way we solve some of the world's most pressing issues.

In short, Willow doesn't just improve upon its predecessors—it completely redefines the concept of **scaling up** in quantum systems. The self-correcting grid of qubits ensures that, as the system grows, its reliability grows too, offering a glimpse into a future where quantum computing is not just powerful but **practical**.

Chapter 4: A New Dimension in Quantum Stability

As quantum systems continue to evolve and grow in complexity, one of the most persistent challenges remains the difficulty of maintaining the fragile quantum properties that make these systems so powerful. Quantum computing operates on the principles of quantum mechanics, and the strange behaviors of qubits—such as superposition and entanglement—are what allow quantum computers to solve problems in ways that classical computers cannot. However, these very same properties that make quantum computing so promising are also what make scaling these systems incredibly difficult.

The main issue lies in the **fragility of quantum states**. Unlike classical bits, which exist in a clear state of either 0 or 1, qubits can exist in multiple states at once due to superposition. This ability allows quantum computers to process vast amounts of information simultaneously. However, qubits are also highly susceptible to **decoherence**, which occurs when quantum states are disturbed by external factors, causing them to lose their quantum properties and behave like classical bits. In a large quantum system, this process becomes even more pronounced as the number of qubits increases. Simply put, the more qubits you have, the harder it is to keep them in their delicate quantum states.

One of the reasons why scaling quantum systems is so difficult is that **bigger doesn't always mean better** in the quantum world. In traditional computing, adding more processors or memory typically results in better performance. But in quantum systems, adding more qubits doesn't necessarily lead to an increase in computational power. Instead, it can result in **greater instability**. As you introduce more qubits, the number of potential interactions between them grows exponentially, making the system more prone to errors. Small disturbances—such as electromagnetic radiation, temperature fluctuations, or even vibrations—can cause qubits to lose their quantum properties and produce incorrect results.

Moreover, traditional methods of error correction used in classical computing don't work well in the quantum realm. Quantum error correction requires a fundamentally different approach because quantum information is inherently **non-classical**. It can't be copied or duplicated in the same way as classical information, meaning that we can't simply back up data to prevent errors. Instead, quantum computers require specialized techniques to detect and correct errors in real-time, which becomes increasingly difficult as the system grows. The larger the quantum system, the harder it is to maintain the coherence of the qubits and to prevent them from becoming corrupted.

This is where most of the challenges in quantum computing arise. It's not just about adding more qubits; it's about keeping them **entangled** and in a state of superposition while avoiding the **quantum noise** that can easily distort the results. As systems scale up, the sheer complexity of these interactions makes it harder to maintain the integrity of the quantum computations. In fact, many quantum systems start to lose their potential power the larger they get because the **quantum properties degrade** as the system becomes more complex.

One of the ways researchers have tried to overcome these challenges is by using error correction schemes. These are designed to detect and fix errors without collapsing the fragile quantum states of the qubits. However, current error correction techniques are still **resource-intensive** and difficult to implement, particularly as the scale of the quantum system grows. The trade-off is that these systems require a lot more physical qubits to perform error correction on a smaller number of logical qubits, leading to even more complexity and, often, a diminishing return on the additional qubits.

But the real breakthrough, as exemplified by **Google's Willow**, is in finding ways to **sustain quantum properties as systems expand**—to make scaling up not only possible but also efficient. Willow's self-correcting mechanism represents a significant step forward in solving this problem. Unlike traditional quantum systems, where increasing the number of qubits often results in instability and error accumulation, Willow introduces an innovative way to handle errors at scale, which allows the system to remain reliable even as the qubit count grows.

Ultimately, the challenge of scaling quantum systems boils down to **preserving quantum coherence** and preventing errors from snowballing as the system expands. The larger a quantum system becomes, the more likely it is to experience issues like decoherence and quantum noise, which can make the system unreliable. However, with new approaches like Willow's self-correcting grid, there is a growing sense that these challenges can be overcome, enabling quantum systems to scale to a size that was previously unimaginable. With these innovations, quantum computers may soon be able to solve some of the most complex problems in physics, chemistry, and beyond, unlocking a new era of computing.

Willow's solution to the problem of scaling quantum systems while maintaining stability represents a revolutionary step forward in the field of quantum computing. For years, quantum researchers have struggled with the fundamental challenge that increasing the size of a quantum computer often leads to a loss of coherence. The more qubits a system has, the harder it becomes to keep them stable. This is because quantum systems are highly sensitive to their environment, and small disturbances can cause qubits to lose their quantum properties, leading to errors and inefficiencies. However, Willow's design and architecture offer a fresh approach to this issue, maintaining the delicate balance needed to preserve quantum coherence even as the system grows.

At the heart of Willow's innovation is its ability to scale up while **preserving the integrity of its quantum properties**. Typically, as a quantum computer increases in size, the interactions between qubits multiply, increasing the likelihood of errors and decoherence. Willow, however, has introduced a sophisticated error-correction mechanism that ensures quantum coherence is not only maintained but actively stabilized. This is achieved by leveraging an advanced technique of **self-correction** that allows the system to grow larger without the errors becoming unmanageable.

What sets Willow apart is its **scalability**. Traditional quantum systems face a trade-off when it comes to scaling: the more qubits you add, the more complex the system becomes, and the more likely it is that the qubits will lose their quantum properties. In Willow's case, this paradox is broken by its self-correcting quantum system. This breakthrough ensures that even as Willow scales up, the qubits remain stable and operational. This is achieved by a **robust error-correction scheme** that doesn't just fix problems but anticipates them before they cause major issues. Willow's grid-like structure helps to distribute errors across the system in a controlled manner, which makes them easier to manage as the system expands.

The concept of **stability paradox**—the challenge of keeping quantum coherence intact while scaling up—is well-known among quantum physicists. According to quantum mechanics, the larger the quantum system, the more interactions between qubits there are, and the more sensitive the system becomes to external influences. This has led to the assumption that large-scale quantum systems would inevitably suffer from **increased instability**. However, Willow challenges this assumption by demonstrating that with the right error-correction framework, **larger systems can actually be more stable**.

In essence, Willow has found a way to break one of the fundamental rules of quantum mechanics: the idea that larger quantum systems are inherently more prone to errors and decoherence. By integrating a **self-correcting mechanism** into its architecture, Willow is able to absorb and fix errors more efficiently, allowing the system to scale without losing its quantum coherence. This is a fundamental shift in how we think about quantum computing, and it opens up new possibilities for what quantum computers can achieve.

To understand the significance of this development, imagine a large team of workers working on a project. As the team grows, you would expect the number of mistakes or miscommunications to increase, making it harder to manage the work. However, if there was a mechanism in place that automatically corrected these mistakes as they happened, the team would remain productive and efficient, no matter how large it grew. In the case of Willow, this self-correcting mechanism allows the quantum system to grow and scale without the usual downsides of instability, ensuring that the qubits stay entangled and operational, even as the system becomes more complex.

This ability to **maintain quantum coherence** at scale is a huge leap forward in the field of quantum computing. As researchers and companies around the world race to build larger and more powerful quantum computers, Willow's breakthrough offers a glimpse into a future where quantum systems can grow in both size and complexity without losing their power. By **stabilizing quantum properties at scale**, Willow not only pushes the boundaries of what is technically possible but also opens the door to practical, large-scale quantum computing that could one day solve some of the world's most complex problems.

Chapter 5: The Speed of Willow: Faster Than the Universe

The speed at which quantum computers operate, particularly Willow, is nothing short of astounding. In the world of traditional computing, speed has always been a major factor in determining the capabilities of a system. Supercomputers, for example, have been the gold standard when it comes to tackling some of the most complex and computationally intensive problems. These machines, built to handle trillions of operations per second, have been employed in fields ranging from climate modeling to drug discovery. Yet, despite their immense power, supercomputers still face significant limitations when it comes to certain types of calculations—limitations that quantum computers like Willow are poised to overcome.

Willow's quantum processors represent a monumental leap in computational speed. Benchmarks of Willow's performance show it solving problems in **minutes** that would otherwise take traditional supercomputers **millennia**. The speed differential between quantum and classical systems is staggering. In fact, calculations that would take supercomputers an unfathomable amount of time—on the order of **10^{25} years**—can now be completed in **under 5 minutes** using Willow's quantum capabilities. This isn't just a marginal improvement; it's a radical shift in the computational landscape, one that redefines what is possible in terms of solving the most complex problems.

To understand just how mind-boggling this difference is, consider the time scales involved. Traditional supercomputers are limited by the physical constraints of classical computing. They perform operations using bits, which can represent either a 0 or a 1. While these systems can operate at extraordinary speeds, their processing power is still fundamentally limited by the need to process these individual bits in a linear fashion. This means that even though supercomputers can perform billions or trillions of calculations per second, they still face a limit when it comes to more complex or large-scale problems.

In contrast, quantum computers like Willow operate using **qubits**, which can represent both 0 and 1 simultaneously due to the principles of **superposition**. This means that Willow can process a vast number of possibilities in parallel, enabling it to tackle problems in a fraction of the time it would take a classical supercomputer. The sheer **speed advantage** here is not just a matter of faster processors—it's a matter of fundamentally different computation methods that open up entirely new avenues for problem-solving.

To further visualize the scale of this speed difference, imagine a task that takes a supercomputer **millions of years** to complete. Now, envision that same task being finished by Willow in just **5 minutes**. The quantum computer doesn't just speed up the process—it fundamentally redefines how quickly a problem can be solved. The implications for industries that rely on complex calculations, such as **drug discovery**, **cryptography**, and **material science**, are profound. Problems that were once considered unsolvable or too time-consuming for traditional systems are now within reach, thanks to Willow's unprecedented speed.

The **astonishing speed** of Willow's quantum computation is not just a technological feat—it's a window into the future of computing. As the potential of quantum systems continues to unfold, we are on the cusp of a new era where complex computations that once seemed impossible are now achievable in seconds, minutes, or hours, rather than millennia. The implications of this breakthrough are limitless, with the potential to unlock new solutions to some of the world's most pressing challenges, from climate change and disease prevention to artificial intelligence and beyond.

What's truly remarkable is that Willow is not just fast—it's **efficient**. It uses the unique properties of quantum mechanics to handle calculations in a way that traditional systems simply cannot replicate. This combination of speed and efficiency makes Willow a true game-changer in the world of computation, and it's just the beginning of what quantum computing can achieve.

The speed at which Willow operates represents far more than a technological achievement; it signals a **profound shift** in how we approach the world's most complex problems. For industries and future technologies, the implications of quantum computing are nothing short of revolutionary. Where traditional systems have been constrained by the laws of classical physics and the limitations of bits, Willow's quantum capabilities shatter those boundaries, enabling industries to explore new frontiers and tackle challenges that were previously considered insurmountable.

To understand the true significance of this speed, it's important to recognize the **exponential gap** that quantum computing opens up between classical and quantum systems. In many domains, this is not just a matter of incremental improvement—it's a leap into entirely new possibilities. Take, for example, fields like **pharmaceutical research**, **cryptography**, and **material science**. These industries often rely on simulations and calculations to model incredibly complex systems, such as the behavior of molecules, the structure of proteins, or the encryption of sensitive data. In the classical world, these computations are immensely time-consuming and sometimes impractical to carry out on a meaningful scale.

Imagine a pharmaceutical company working to discover new drugs to combat a global health crisis. Traditional supercomputers, despite their impressive power, can still take weeks or months to simulate the interactions of a single molecule or analyze a single drug compound. But with Willow's quantum computing power, tasks like these can be accomplished **in minutes** or even **seconds**. The sheer speed difference means that researchers could run thousands of simulations in the time it would take a classical system to process just one. This opens up a new world of possibilities for drug discovery, where insights that once took years to gather might now be available in a matter of weeks, or even days.

In **cryptography**, Willow's ability to process vast amounts of data with lightning speed could revolutionize the security of communications. While classical encryption methods rely on the difficulty of certain mathematical problems (like factoring large numbers), quantum computers can solve these problems in a fraction of the time, potentially rendering current encryption methods obsolete. But the same speed also offers new ways of **securing information**. Quantum encryption techniques, which rely on the principles of quantum mechanics, promise to be virtually unbreakable, providing a new layer of protection for sensitive data. This quantum leap in security could change the landscape of online privacy, corporate security, and government communications.

Material science is another field that will feel the impact of quantum computing. The ability to simulate complex chemical reactions at an unprecedented scale could lead to the discovery of new materials with remarkable properties—perhaps materials that are more energy-efficient, lighter, or more durable than anything we have today. Willow's ability to simulate these materials in a fraction of the time it would take classical systems could accelerate the development of **next-generation technologies** like better batteries, advanced electronics, or even materials for space exploration.

Beyond these industries, the **exponential gap** between classical and quantum computation will also have a profound effect on the broader development of **artificial intelligence (AI)**. Machine learning algorithms, which are already transforming everything from healthcare to finance, rely on enormous amounts of data and complex computations to make predictions and uncover insights. As quantum computers like Willow advance, AI could enter a new era where learning and adaptation happen at speeds and scales that were previously unimaginable. **Deep learning** and **neural networks**, which already show great promise, could reach new heights with the power of quantum systems, making machines smarter and more capable of solving problems that were once thought too complex for computers.

In essence, the leap beyond classical computing that Willow represents is not just a matter of solving problems faster; it's about solving problems that were **once deemed unsolvable**. The speed and power of quantum systems like Willow make possible breakthroughs that extend far beyond the reach of current technologies. It's a

game-changer for a variety of industries, and it's just the beginning. As these systems scale up and mature, we can only begin to imagine the new innovations and advances that will reshape the world.

Chapter 6: Will Quantum Computing Break Bitcoin?

The emergence of quantum computing has generated a mixture of excitement and concern, particularly in the realm of cryptocurrency. One of the most frequently asked questions is whether quantum computers like Willow will be able to break the encryption that secures Bitcoin and other cryptocurrencies. After all, quantum computers possess **immense computational power**—power that could potentially surpass the capabilities of current cryptographic systems. But before panic sets in, it's important to address the myths surrounding this issue and provide clarity on why quantum computers, including Willow, aren't the immediate threat some might believe.

Let's start by understanding the core of the concern. **Bitcoin's security relies on cryptographic techniques** that are designed to be difficult to crack using classical computers. The main method of securing Bitcoin transactions is a process called

public-key cryptography, specifically using the **Elliptic Curve Digital Signature Algorithm (ECDSA)**. The concern is that a sufficiently powerful quantum computer could perform what's called a **Shor's Algorithm** to quickly factor large numbers and break this encryption, potentially exposing Bitcoin wallets and compromising transactions.

At first glance, this might sound alarming. After all, quantum computers are capable of solving certain problems exponentially faster than classical computers. However, the complexity of breaking Bitcoin's security is **not just about speed**; it's about the way in which quantum computers are built and the specific types of computations they excel at. Here's where the confusion often lies. While quantum computers do indeed outperform classical computers in certain tasks, they aren't necessarily equipped to break every type of encryption.

The first myth we need to debunk is the idea that **Willow**, or any quantum computer, is immediately ready to crack Bitcoin's security. In reality, **Willow is still in its early stages of development**. While it's an incredibly powerful quantum processor, its primary focus is not on **cracking encryption** or solving the types of cryptographic puzzles Bitcoin uses. Willow's breakthroughs are more about **error correction**, scalability, and quantum coherence—far removed from the specialized algorithms required to threaten Bitcoin's encryption.

But let's address the question of **Willow's speed** and the complexity of breaking Bitcoin's security. One useful analogy here is comparing Willow to a **Ferrari**. While the Ferrari is undeniably fast, it's designed for a different purpose than, say, a rugged 4x4 off-road vehicle. The Ferrari is built for speed on a paved highway, not for navigating the unpredictable terrain of cryptographic algorithms. In other words, while Willow has the capability to perform certain types of calculations much faster than traditional computers, this doesn't mean it is automatically suited for the kind of attack needed to break Bitcoin's security.

Quantum computers like Willow are specialized tools designed for **particular kinds of problems**. The algorithms used to attack Bitcoin's security are not just about raw computational speed. They require a specific kind of quantum algorithm, and even with Willow's speed, **Bitcoin's cryptographic systems would need a new type of quantum attack** to be vulnerable. This kind of attack hasn't been developed yet, and there's no immediate sign that Willow or other current quantum systems are close to posing a threat.

Furthermore, Bitcoin's network and the wider cryptocurrency ecosystem are already **anticipating the quantum future**. Researchers are actively working on developing **quantum-resistant algorithms**—also known as

post-quantum cryptography—that would be able to withstand the power of quantum computers like Willow. These new encryption systems are designed to be resistant to quantum attacks, which means that as quantum computing progresses, Bitcoin's encryption can evolve along with it. In fact, Bitcoin's community and developers are already exploring ways to implement quantum-resistant algorithms, which would protect the network long before quantum computers could pose any real threat.

To understand this better, imagine you're **upgrading your house's security system** in anticipation of a new type of burglar that's still in the design phase. You don't need to wait for the burglar to actually arrive; you can update your system proactively, ensuring that your house remains safe even against advanced threats. This is essentially what the cryptocurrency community is doing: **preparing for the quantum future before it arrives**.

In summary, while the rise of quantum computing, and Willow in particular, may seem like it poses a threat to Bitcoin's encryption, the reality is far more nuanced. Quantum computers like Willow, at least for now, are not designed to crack Bitcoin's encryption, and even if they were, the community is already working on post-quantum solutions. Rather than fearing quantum computing as a direct threat, we should recognize that it is likely to be a catalyst for innovation—driving the development of more **secure, quantum-resistant systems** that will keep cryptocurrencies and digital currencies safe for years to come.

So, while Willow and its successors will undoubtedly change the landscape of computing and cryptography, they are not the immediate menace to Bitcoin's security that some might fear. Instead, they are part of the ongoing evolution of technology, where each step forward brings both new challenges and new opportunities for progress.

As the world moves towards increasingly advanced forms of computing, one area that has garnered significant attention is **cryptography**—the art and science of securing information. With the rise of quantum computers, there is a growing concern about the future of cryptographic systems, particularly how quantum computing might impact the security mechanisms that keep our digital lives safe. The question is no longer a matter of **if** quantum computing will affect cryptography but rather **when** and **how** it will happen.

To understand this, it's important to first appreciate how current encryption methods work. Today's cryptographic systems rely heavily on **mathematical problems that are easy to solve in one direction but extremely difficult to reverse.** For instance, **public-key cryptography**, which underpins systems like Bitcoin, is based on the difficulty of factoring large prime numbers or solving elliptic curve problems. These problems are designed to be incredibly difficult for classical computers to solve, even with vast amounts of computational power. This is what keeps systems like Bitcoin and most digital transactions secure today.

However, quantum computers operate on fundamentally different principles than classical computers. They use **qubits**, which, thanks to quantum mechanics, can exist in multiple states at once. This ability to perform multiple calculations simultaneously gives quantum computers the potential to solve certain problems **exponentially faster** than classical computers. For cryptography, this presents a serious challenge. If quantum computers become powerful enough, they could break the encryption schemes that have protected everything from online banking to government communications. Specifically, a quantum computer could use **Shor's Algorithm**, a quantum algorithm that efficiently factors large numbers, potentially rendering traditional encryption methods obsolete.

For now, quantum computers like Willow are still in the early stages of development, but they are advancing rapidly. It's clear that their impact on cryptography in the future will be profound. While current systems are secure against classical computers, they could eventually become vulnerable to quantum-enabled attacks. As a result, the cryptography community has been working on what's known as **post-quantum cryptography**—encryption methods that are designed to be secure against both classical and quantum threats.

The advent of post-quantum cryptography is not just a theoretical necessity. It is becoming a practical imperative. Experts predict that it may only be a matter of time before quantum computers are powerful enough to break existing encryption systems. This means that all of today's encryption methods—everything from the encryption used in credit card transactions to the systems securing government data—need to evolve. These systems must be **future-proof** to withstand the capabilities of quantum computing.

One of the biggest challenges is the **transition period**. It's not enough to simply wait for quantum computers to arrive and then switch to new encryption methods. Cryptographic systems are deeply embedded in every aspect of modern life. Changing the encryption standards for something as fundamental as securing banking transactions or personal data is a massive undertaking. This is why the **shift to quantum-resistant encryption** needs to begin now, well before quantum computers are fully capable of breaking current systems. Governments, tech companies, and cryptographers around the world are already testing and developing new encryption algorithms that are designed to be immune to quantum attacks.

For instance, **lattice-based cryptography** is one of the most promising areas of post-quantum cryptography. Lattice problems are considered hard even for quantum computers to solve, making them ideal candidates for future-proof encryption systems. Researchers are also exploring **hash-based signatures** and **code-based cryptography**, both of which show promise in resisting quantum decryption techniques. By focusing on these and other quantum-resistant algorithms, cryptography will not only survive the advent of quantum computing but will evolve to become even more secure and robust than it is today.

The timeline for this transition is crucial. We are still several years away from quantum computers being powerful enough to break current cryptographic systems, but that doesn't mean we should wait until the last moment to make the switch. In fact, it may take **decades** for new cryptographic standards to be widely adopted and integrated into every system that relies on encryption. The reality is that by the time quantum computers are mature enough to crack traditional cryptography, many of today's systems could already be outdated or insecure without the necessary updates.

To put it simply, the future of cryptography isn't about being reactive to quantum computing—it's about **anticipating and preparing for the quantum future**. This involves developing and implementing encryption systems that are resistant to quantum attacks and ensuring that they are ready well before quantum computers become a real threat. This ongoing work will secure the digital infrastructure that supports everything from our online transactions to our personal communications.

As we look toward the future, it's important to remember that **quantum computing won't just be an obstacle to overcome—it will also drive innovation**. While there are significant challenges in ensuring the security of digital systems in the age of quantum computing, there are also **opportunities for growth**. Post-quantum cryptography, once fully developed and implemented, will not only keep us safe from quantum threats but will also **lay the foundation for the next generation of secure technologies**, potentially opening up new realms of possibility in everything from online privacy to secure cloud computing.

In conclusion, the future of cryptography is at a crossroads. The rise of quantum computing presents a challenge that is undeniable, but it also sparks the **innovation necessary to future-proof our systems**. With the right advancements in cryptography, we can ensure that the digital world remains secure in the age of quantum computing, preserving the privacy, security, and integrity of the vast amount of information we rely on every day. The road ahead is one of transformation, but it's a transformation we must embrace to safeguard our future.

Chapter 7: Could Quantum Computers Tap into Parallel Universes?

The concept of **parallel universes** has long captivated the human imagination, appearing in science fiction, philosophical discussions, and even speculative scientific theories. But what if quantum computing, the cutting-edge technology we're so eager to harness, could unlock the doors to these alternate realities? The idea is so mind-bending that it almost sounds like something out of a science fiction novel. Yet, as quantum computing advances, some scientists and theorists have begun to explore the possibility that quantum computers might not only work in our universe—they could, in some sense, tap into the very fabric of multiple realities, operating in ways that defy our traditional understanding of time and space.

To understand this, it's essential to grasp the unusual principles that govern quantum mechanics. At the heart of quantum physics lies the concept of **superposition**, which allows quantum particles to exist in multiple states simultaneously. Rather than having one definitive position, quantum particles can be in multiple places, with different energies or spins, until they are measured or observed. This idea of multiple states existing at once is one of the fundamental mysteries of quantum mechanics, and it has prompted physicists to ask some very unusual questions: **What if these states represent different realities or universes, all co-existing?**

This is where things begin to get really fascinating. If quantum computers are harnessing the power of qubits, which exist in superpositions, could they be processing information across these multiple realities? Some theories suggest that quantum computing might not just involve manipulating information within a single universe but could be a form of **parallel processing across multiple realities**. In this scenario, the quantum computer could be tapping into different timelines, universes, or realities, all operating simultaneously to solve problems much faster and more efficiently than classical computers.

One theory, known as the **Many-Worlds Interpretation** of quantum mechanics, posits that every time a quantum measurement is made, the universe "splits" into multiple branches, each representing a different outcome. Each of these branches would be its own separate universe, with its own distinct timeline. If this theory holds, then it's possible that quantum computers might be able to compute not just in our universe but across a multitude of parallel universes, each of which holds a potential outcome of every quantum computation.

Imagine, then, that each qubit in a quantum computer represents not just one state of information, but **several states**, each corresponding to a different version of reality. By leveraging the phenomenon of **entanglement**, where qubits become linked in ways that defy classical physics, quantum computers might be able to solve problems that involve navigating these realities—problems that are too complex for classical computers to even attempt.

If this theory is true, it would mean that quantum computers could, in a very real sense, be **computing across parallel worlds**. This kind of computing wouldn't just involve calculations happening in a single space-time continuum; it would involve multiple, interconnected dimensions. Each qubit's state could represent the outcome of different possibilities from different universes, and by processing all of these simultaneously, quantum computers could arrive at solutions that we could never have conceived of using traditional computing.

To put this idea into perspective, think of it as trying to solve a maze. A traditional computer might explore one path at a time, trying each possibility sequentially until it finds the solution. But a quantum computer, using superposition and entanglement, might explore **all possible paths at once**, in multiple parallel realities, rapidly converging on the solution in a fraction of the time it would take a classical computer to check each one individually. In essence, quantum computation would be like solving a problem **across multiple timelines at the same time**—a form of **parallel processing** that leverages the power of the multiverse.

Of course, this remains highly speculative, and much of it exists on the fringe of theoretical physics. But as quantum computing continues to evolve, some researchers are increasingly open to the possibility that quantum mechanics is far more mysterious than we have yet realized. The idea of parallel universes is no longer confined to the realm of science fiction; it's now an active area of scientific debate, one that could change the very way we think about computation and the fabric of reality itself.

This theory also raises profound questions about the nature of information. If quantum computers are, in a sense, **communicating across realities**, does it mean that information is not confined to a single universe, but rather flows freely across the multiverse? Could this open the door to new forms of computing that transcend the physical limitations of our world? Could we, through quantum computation, be tapping into an underlying structure of reality that connects all of existence, allowing us to access new realms of knowledge and understanding?

In the coming years, as we learn more about the true potential of quantum computing, these questions will likely become less abstract and more concrete. **Willow,** with its incredible advancements in quantum technology, is at the forefront of this journey into the unknown. As it pushes the boundaries of what's possible with quantum computing, it could very well lead to discoveries that reveal the interconnectedness of all things, providing a glimpse into a world where the boundaries between universes are far more permeable than we ever imagined.

Whether or not quantum computers will ever access parallel universes is still uncertain, but one thing is clear: the potential of quantum computing stretches far beyond the practical applications we've already seen. As we continue to push the limits of what's possible, quantum computers like Willow could one day open doors to realms of understanding that will forever change the way we think about computation, technology, and perhaps even the very nature of existence itself.

Imagine you're tasked with solving a maze. For most people, the way to approach this challenge is by trial and error, walking down one path at a time, trying to find the exit. You might have to go back to the start several times, retracing your steps, until you figure out which path leads to the solution. This is how classical computers approach problems—they handle one possibility at a time, sifting through countless options sequentially until the right one is found.

Now, picture something radically different. Instead of one person walking the maze, imagine you have a group of people, each at a different entrance or path, each trying different routes simultaneously. Some might find the solution in minutes, while others might take longer, but overall, you have a **multi-pronged approach** that can cover far more ground in a fraction of the time. This is a simplified analogy of how **quantum computers** like Willow work, but with a mind-bending twist: instead of just one maze, there are countless versions of it, each representing a different path, or even a different universe.

This analogy is where the idea of **parallel universes** comes into play. While classical computers work through trial and error, one possibility at a time, quantum computers can potentially explore **all possibilities simultaneously**. This is made possible by the strange principles of **quantum mechanics**—superposition and entanglement—which allow quantum systems to exist in multiple states at once, each corresponding to different versions of the maze or the problem you're trying to solve.

So, let's extend this idea: imagine that instead of just one person trying the maze, there are multiple versions of you, each in a parallel universe, each walking a different path simultaneously. All of you are connected through **quantum entanglement**, which means that no matter where you are in your separate universes, you can still "share information" and coordinate efforts. Every version of you is working together, solving different aspects of the problem at the same time. This is like the **quantum computer's qubits**—each qubit can exist in a superposition of states, processing information across multiple realities simultaneously, rather than just one possibility at a time.

For Willow, this means that it could be processing an **enormous amount of possibilities** all at once—essentially tackling a multi-dimensional problem in ways that traditional computers simply cannot. Where classical computers would try each path individually, taking countless steps and running through iterations, Willow might be solving the maze **simultaneously across multiple timelines**, with its qubits acting like explorers in parallel universes, each uncovering a different part of the solution at the same time.

In more technical terms, Willow's **quantum superposition** allows it to hold multiple states at once. The more qubits it has, the more potential states it can explore simultaneously. This means Willow could be solving problems **exponentially faster** than classical computers because it's not just solving a problem one step at a time; it's working on every possible step at once. And thanks to the quantum phenomenon of **entanglement**, all of these paths can be correlated in a way that ensures the correct solution emerges without having to sift through every possibility manually.

To visualize this on a larger scale: imagine that the maze you're trying to solve has billions of pathways. A classical computer would test each one, trying and discarding paths until it finds the exit. For Willow, however, each of its qubits can be in a superposition of all possible paths, allowing it to try **every pathway at the same time**. Instead of taking a lifetime to solve the maze, Willow could potentially finish the task in just moments, depending on the complexity.

This is where the idea of **parallel universes** comes into play. What's really mind-blowing is that these multiple versions of Willow's qubits aren't just "imaginary" or theoretical—they could represent **parallel realities** where each reality is trying a different path or computing a different possibility at the same time. This doesn't mean that Willow is literally jumping through multiple dimensions, but in the quantum world, the computation itself could be spread across what seem like "parallel universes," each representing a different branch of reality.

In essence, Willow is like a group of explorers, each one with their own set of skills, each in a different version of the maze, each contributing their findings in real-time to the solution. It's not bound by the limitations of classical computing, where **bigger systems mean more instability** or slower processing times. Instead, Willow's **quantum properties** allow it to handle these vast, parallel explorations with **unprecedented speed and efficiency**, solving problems **millions of times faster** than any classical machine could hope to achieve.

This ability to tap into multiple possibilities at once is one of the core advantages of quantum computing. Where classical computers are limited to testing one hypothesis at a time, Willow could process **all possible scenarios at the same time**, dramatically reducing the time it takes to solve even the most complex problems. And just like the maze analogy, Willow's speed isn't just about solving the problem faster—it's about solving it in a fundamentally different way, accessing realities that were previously unimaginable, allowing for a solution to emerge from the **quantum fabric of the universe itself**.

Chapter 8: What's Next? The Roadmap to Quantum Supremacy

For years, we have been locked into the constraints of classical computing, where the speed of processing is limited by the number of bits, the fundamental units of information. These bits are binary, meaning they can only exist in one of two states: 0 or 1. While this simplicity has served humanity well for decades, it also means that certain complex problems are inherently difficult or even impossible for classical computers to solve within a reasonable time frame. This limitation has been a defining characteristic of the digital age. But now, with the advent of quantum computing, that limitation is being challenged, and in some cases, outright shattered.

Willow represents a monumental leap in this new quantum frontier. One of the most remarkable achievements of quantum computing, and specifically Willow, is its ability to tackle problems that classical systems simply cannot. These are the problems that have remained unsolved for decades, due to the sheer number of variables or the level of complexity involved—problems like simulating the behavior of molecules at the quantum level, optimizing global supply chains, or cracking the toughest encryption algorithms. For classical computers, these problems would take millennia to solve. For Willow, they are within reach.

Willow's first major milestone was proving that a quantum computer could outperform a classical one in a specific, meaningful task—a feat known as **quantum supremacy**. Google achieved this feat with its earlier quantum processor, **Sycamore**, but Willow goes even further. With its superior error correction and stability, Willow has made it possible to solve these otherwise insurmountable problems in a fraction of the time it would take a classical supercomputer. This is not a theoretical possibility anymore; it's a tangible breakthrough that signals the dawn of a new computational age.

Willow's success in this milestone was not just about speed—it was about demonstrating that quantum computing is no longer a theoretical exercise. It can actually **do things classical computers cannot**. For instance, it has shown promise in **quantum chemistry simulations**, a task that classical computers struggle with due to the complexity of modeling molecular structures. In traditional computing, the problem grows exponentially as the molecules get more complex. But Willow, thanks to its qubits, is able to process these multiple interactions simultaneously and at much higher efficiencies, leading to faster and more accurate simulations.

Willow's achievement is also significant in the world of **optimization problems**, which are at the heart of everything from logistics to machine learning. The ability to solve optimization problems more efficiently can revolutionize industries by helping them find the most effective solutions faster—whether it's scheduling flights, managing production lines, or even tackling environmental issues like climate modeling. Where classical computers would take weeks or months to find an optimal solution, Willow is able to compute the possibilities much faster, cutting down both time and resource consumption.

Beyond the technical achievements, Willow's success marks the beginning of a **paradigm shift** in computing. It's no longer about squeezing more processing power into smaller and smaller chips. Instead, it's about harnessing the strange, probabilistic power of quantum mechanics itself. And with each milestone Willow reaches, it not only proves that quantum computers can outperform classical ones, but it also opens doors to new realms of possibility—possibilities that will change the fabric of technology, AI, and even human understanding of the universe.

In many ways, Willow's success is just the beginning. By demonstrating that quantum computing can achieve things beyond the grasp of classical systems, Willow has set the stage for a future where these quantum computers will be able to solve more practical, real-world problems that we haven't even thought of yet. This is a step beyond "theoretical" or "possible"—it's now about **achievable and real**, and Willow is leading the way into that reality.

Quantum computing has long been considered one of the most revolutionary advancements in technology, but its promise has been held back by a significant hurdle: **quantum error correction**. Unlike classical systems, which rely on simple, deterministic binary states (0 or 1), quantum systems operate on qubits that can exist in multiple states simultaneously—a phenomenon known as **superposition**. This gives quantum computers their incredible processing power. However, this same property also makes them extremely susceptible to errors, as qubits are easily disturbed by external factors such as temperature fluctuations, electromagnetic interference, or even cosmic radiation. This is where error correction becomes crucial.

Traditional computing has long been familiar with error correction methods, like parity checks and redundancy, which detect and correct mistakes that occur during computation. In quantum computing, however, the situation is far more complex. A single error can unravel the delicate balance of qubits, causing the entire computation to fail. Until recently, this issue made it extremely difficult to scale quantum systems beyond a handful of qubits. The idea of building large, stable quantum computers seemed like a distant dream, as any increase in the number of qubits led to an increase in errors, making computations unreliable.

But Willow has made a monumental leap forward in quantum error correction. **Error correction in Willow is not merely about fixing mistakes as they happen**; it's about creating a system that can **anticipate and prevent errors** from impacting the computational results, even as the quantum system grows in size and complexity. Through its innovative self-correcting mechanisms, Willow ensures that it can **maintain the integrity of quantum information**, even when subjected to significant noise or external disruptions. This is where Willow stands apart from its predecessors, setting a new standard for the quantum computing world.

One of the key features that makes Willow's error correction so revolutionary is its ability to use an **increasing number of qubits in tandem** to manage and correct errors. In earlier quantum systems, adding more qubits would often amplify the risk of errors, as the system struggled to maintain coherence as it scaled. Willow, on the other hand, employs a strategy that **enhances its error correction abilities** as it adds more qubits, allowing it to grow without compromising the stability of the system.

This breakthrough is akin to a team of workers tasked with fixing errors in a massive building project. As the team expands, it's not just about more workers doing the same thing—it's about organizing the workforce in a way that each worker can manage a specific part of the problem, ensuring that each task is done efficiently and that any mistakes are caught and corrected before they cause significant issues. The larger the team, the more mistakes can be caught and corrected in parallel, and the more stable the overall project becomes. This is how Willow's error-correction system works—scaling with its computational power while improving its error-handling capabilities.

Furthermore, Willow's **error-correction grid** is an extraordinary advance. Rather than using a simple error-detecting system, Willow's architecture incorporates sophisticated redundancy measures to detect, identify, and correct errors within its quantum circuits. This is done by organizing qubits into a **grid structure** that grows in size as the quantum system expands. In its simplest form, Willow's error-correction mechanism works by employing a small 3x3 grid, but as the system scales, the grid grows to 5x5 and eventually to 7x7, allowing for increasingly accurate and resilient computations.

This innovation is what allows Willow to scale effectively without sacrificing performance. It's a key element in allowing quantum computing to transition from theoretical research to a practical and operational technology capable of solving real-world problems. Without this capability to handle errors efficiently, Willow would be no more than an interesting prototype—an idea that couldn't be made to work reliably in practice.

The development of robust quantum error correction is a game-changer for the entire quantum computing field. With these advancements, Willow is **paving the way for future quantum systems** that will be capable of reliably performing calculations on a larger scale, solving problems that were previously considered impossible or impractical. This stability, coupled with the immense power of quantum computation, is what will enable industries—from healthcare to logistics, to AI and cryptography—to harness the true potential of quantum systems. Willow's achievement in this area is not just about making things work; it's about making things work **consistently** and **reliably**, and that is what will drive the future of quantum computing.

The quest for building **long-lived logical qubits** is one of the greatest challenges in quantum computing, and it represents a critical milestone on the road to truly powerful quantum systems. Qubits, unlike classical bits, don't simply exist in a state of 0 or 1; they exist in a quantum superposition of both, allowing quantum computers to solve complex problems exponentially faster than classical systems. However, this unique property comes at a cost: **quantum decoherence**.

Quantum decoherence refers to the loss of the delicate quantum state that allows qubits to perform their extraordinary computational feats.

Qubits are inherently fragile, and even slight disturbances—such as temperature changes, electromagnetic interference, or stray vibrations—can cause them to lose their quantum properties and collapse into a classical state. This is why many early quantum computers could only perform very short calculations before their qubits "decayed," rendering their computations unreliable.

The race towards creating **logical qubits**—which are far more stable and durable than their raw physical counterparts—has been one of the defining battles in quantum computing. A logical qubit is a higher-level construct that doesn't rely on the fragile properties of a single physical qubit. Instead, it is built by encoding information across multiple physical qubits, creating a system that can withstand errors and maintain stability over longer periods. The aim is to create qubits that are not only stable but also last long enough to perform the lengthy and complex calculations required to solve real-world problems. This has been a

long-standing hurdle in the quantum world, as no qubit has been stable enough to carry out the kinds of computations necessary for large-scale quantum systems.

For a while, creating long-lived qubits was thought to be an insurmountable problem. Traditional quantum computers relied on qubits that decayed rapidly, causing the quantum system to fail after just a few operations. But now, thanks to advancements like Willow, the concept of **logical qubits** that can endure longer than ever before is becoming a reality. Willow's innovative approach to building logical qubits is a huge leap forward, as it pushes the boundaries of what's possible in quantum systems.

The key to Willow's success lies in its **error-correction mechanisms** and **quantum coherence preservation techniques**, which allow it to maintain qubit stability for longer periods without succumbing to the decaying process that typically hampers quantum systems.

The logical qubits in Willow are designed to be more resistant to environmental interference and to **maintain their quantum state longer**, enabling the system to perform more complex and accurate calculations without being interrupted by errors or decoherence.

In essence, Willow is not just building **quantum computers**; it's **creating the building blocks of a new quantum era** where logical qubits can be scaled up, maintained over time, and used to solve real-world problems across various industries. This is an absolutely pivotal moment in the journey of quantum computing. Once the issue of **long-lived qubits** is solved, the possibilities for quantum systems become virtually limitless. This breakthrough will enable **quantum systems to perform long-term, stable calculations** that could previously only be dreamed of—like simulating complex molecules for pharmaceutical research, optimizing supply chains, or tackling intractable problems in AI.

Willow's milestone in building long-lived logical qubits doesn't just represent a **technical achievement**; it also signals that **quantum computing is finally ready for the big leagues**. The industry has been waiting for years to see if quantum systems could break free from their instability, and Willow is showing the world that it is no longer just a matter of hope—it's a matter of reality.

Quantum gates are the fundamental building blocks of quantum computation. They act like the logic gates in classical computers, but they operate in a completely different way, taking advantage of the strange and powerful properties of quantum mechanics. In classical computing, logic gates like AND, OR, and NOT manipulate bits, flipping them between 0 and 1. Quantum gates, however, manipulate qubits, the quantum counterparts of bits, in ways that allow them to be in a superposition of states, simultaneously holding both 0 and 1. This ability to exist in multiple states at once gives quantum computers their unparalleled potential to solve complex problems.

To perform meaningful computations, a quantum computer needs to apply a series of quantum gates to qubits, constructing what are known as **quantum algorithms**. These algorithms, when designed correctly, can solve problems that are currently intractable for classical computers. For example, quantum algorithms can break encryption, simulate chemical reactions, or optimize complex logistical operations in ways that would have taken classical computers **millennia** to solve. However, the effectiveness of these quantum algorithms relies heavily on the reliability of the quantum gates themselves.

One of the biggest challenges in building a quantum computer is ensuring that these gates operate with perfect precision. In traditional computers, logic gates are incredibly reliable, executing billions of operations without failure. But in quantum systems, the quantum gates must manipulate fragile qubits that are susceptible to interference and errors from the environment. This fragility means that even small errors in quantum gate operations can rapidly compound and lead to a failure of the entire system.

This is where **Willow** stands out. The breakthrough that Willow represents in quantum computing is not just in its qubits, but in the development of **reliable quantum gates**. The quantum gates in Willow are designed to be much more stable and resistant to errors than those of previous systems. They help ensure that the algorithms built on Willow's qubits can operate efficiently and effectively, even as the complexity of the tasks they are trying to solve increases.

For Willow, the ability to apply quantum gates reliably is key to its potential in **AI-powered quantum applications**. Many of the most exciting applications of quantum computing lie in the intersection of AI and quantum mechanics. Quantum computers have the potential to revolutionize artificial intelligence by processing vast amounts of data simultaneously, training models faster, and solving optimization problems that are currently unsolvable with classical machines. But to achieve this, quantum computers must be able to apply complex quantum algorithms without error. This requires highly reliable quantum gates, ones that can perform operations on qubits in a way that doesn't collapse their quantum state prematurely.

In Willow's case, its **reliable quantum gates** represent a critical milestone in making AI-powered quantum applications a reality. By ensuring that quantum gates function with unprecedented precision, Willow opens up new possibilities for AI development. For instance, it could lead to breakthroughs in **machine learning** where quantum computers can analyze patterns in large datasets far quicker than current methods allow. AI-powered drug discovery could also be accelerated, where quantum computers simulate molecular interactions with the speed and accuracy needed for meaningful scientific advancement. The possibilities are endless, and reliable quantum gates are the key to unlocking this potential.

Willow's achievement in building dependable quantum gates is a stepping stone toward a world where **quantum algorithms** and **AI technologies** are seamlessly integrated, giving rise to entirely new industries and capabilities. With quantum gates that function with high fidelity, Willow can handle the most sophisticated algorithms, ushering in a new era where **AI-powered quantum applications** could tackle problems that were once thought impossible. This milestone marks not just the evolution of quantum computing, but the convergence of quantum power and artificial intelligence, setting the stage for breakthroughs that could reshape the world as we know it.

Building a large-scale quantum computer that can solve real-world problems is the ultimate goal of quantum computing, and it's one of the most challenging milestones in the field. For decades, scientists and engineers have been able to demonstrate small-scale quantum systems capable of solving specific problems or proving certain principles. However, scaling up these systems to the level where they can consistently perform complex, meaningful computations in a real-world setting is an entirely different task. This is where **Willow** marks a turning point in the quantum computing journey.

In the past, quantum systems have been limited by a variety of factors, most notably the **fragility** of quantum states and the difficulty of maintaining coherence as the system grows. While a small number of qubits in a controlled environment can perform basic quantum operations, the larger a quantum system gets, the harder it is to keep all the qubits stable, interconnected, and functioning correctly. Traditional approaches to quantum computing often resulted in **high error rates** as the system expanded, making it difficult to perform even moderately complex computations.

The breakthrough of Willow lies in its ability to **scale quantum systems effectively** without losing the integrity of the quantum states. As Willow pushes toward large-scale operation, it builds on the advancements in **quantum error correction** and **quantum gates**, ensuring that it can continue to function at a larger scale. This is an essential step toward building quantum computers that can solve **real-world problems**, not just theoretical ones.

For a quantum system to become genuinely useful in the real world, it needs to be able to **solve problems with practical implications**—problems that have been beyond the reach of classical computers. These problems might include complex simulations for drug discovery, optimization challenges in logistics, or the development of new materials with specific properties. For these applications to work, a quantum system must be able to run long, complex calculations with accuracy and stability, characteristics that have historically been challenging in quantum systems.

Willow's engineers and scientists have overcome many of the barriers that have previously hindered large-scale quantum systems. By applying new methods of **error correction, quantum gate reliability**, and **scalability**, Willow has successfully taken the first steps toward building a **full quantum system** that is not only large in size but also capable of delivering **real-world solutions**. This is the key difference that sets Willow apart from previous quantum systems—its ability to scale up and still produce results that matter outside the laboratory.

One of the challenges of scaling quantum systems is ensuring that the qubits maintain their coherence as the system grows in size. As more qubits are added, the system becomes more susceptible to environmental interference, which can cause the delicate quantum states to collapse prematurely, ruining the computations. Willow addresses this challenge with its **self-correcting quantum system**, which reduces the errors that typically occur as quantum systems scale up. This self-correction mechanism is one of the critical innovations that allow Willow to be the first step toward engineering a quantum computer capable of tackling **real-world problems** at a larger scale.

With Willow's advancement, the dream of building **full quantum systems** that are powerful enough to address industries like **pharmaceuticals, AI, cryptography, and material science** is becoming a reality. The potential applications of this technology are staggering, from speeding up drug discovery to solving problems in optimization and AI that were previously unimaginable. Willow's ability to build **large-scale quantum systems** means that industries can begin to rely on quantum computing as a legitimate tool for solving **real-world problems**.

The road ahead is long, and there are still hurdles to overcome. But Willow's progress marks a major milestone in the journey toward practical, large-scale quantum computing. As these systems mature, the **real-world impact** of quantum computing will only grow, solving problems that were once considered beyond the reach of any computer. For now, Willow stands at the forefront of a new era, with the ability to tackle the most complex challenges in technology, science, and industry. With each milestone it achieves, Willow brings us closer to the world where **quantum systems at scale** become the norm, revolutionizing everything from **AI-driven breakthroughs** to **drug discovery** and beyond.

The pursuit of **artificial superintelligence** has captivated researchers, technologists, and futurists for decades. The idea of creating machines that can think, learn, and evolve beyond human intelligence is both thrilling and daunting. While the concept remains largely theoretical for now, the advancements in quantum computing—especially the breakthroughs achieved with **Willow**—are laying the groundwork for what could be the next monumental leap in artificial intelligence.

At its core, the goal of **artificial superintelligence** is to build a system that can process information, solve problems, and make decisions with a level of complexity and capability far surpassing human abilities. While today's AI systems are already powerful, they are still limited by the constraints of **classical computing**. They rely on algorithms that process data through basic binary operations, which, although efficient for many tasks, struggle to handle the extreme complexity of problems that arise in areas like **medicine**, **climate modeling**, and **advanced robotics**.

This is where **quantum computing** has the potential to truly revolutionize AI. Quantum systems, like Willow, operate based on **quantum**

bits (or qubits) rather than the traditional binary bits used by classical computers. These qubits can exist in multiple states at once, thanks to the principles of **superposition** and **entanglement**. This allows quantum computers to process vast amounts of data and run complex calculations at exponentially faster rates than classical systems. For artificial intelligence, this means the ability to analyze, learn from, and respond to data with a level of sophistication that was previously unimaginable.

The **innovations** made by Willow in quantum computing—particularly in areas like **quantum error correction**, **stability at scale**, and **quantum gate reliability**—are building the foundation for a future where **superintelligent systems** are not just theoretical possibilities but practical, realizable technologies. Willow's ability to scale while maintaining **quantum coherence** makes it possible to harness quantum systems for more than just basic computations. These advancements are paving the way for the development of **quantum-powered AI** systems that could process and understand information at a much deeper level, solve problems in real-time, and adapt to ever-evolving challenges.

The **speed** and **power** that quantum computers like Willow bring to the table will be key in achieving the **artificial superintelligence** that many envision. Unlike classical computers, which take linear time to process information, quantum computers can solve certain types of problems in **parallel**. This allows them to explore vast possibilities and potential solutions simultaneously. Imagine an AI that could analyze the vast interconnectedness of every possible outcome, simultaneously considering multiple future scenarios and optimizing decisions across countless variables—all within moments. This is a level of processing power that classical AI systems simply can't achieve.

But how does Willow specifically contribute to this **superintelligent future**? Its ability to **scale efficiently** while keeping quantum errors in check means that quantum systems will become more and more reliable over time. The precision required to build **logical qubits** that don't decay instantly—what's needed for sustained computation—has been a huge obstacle in the journey toward quantum AI. With Willow's innovative approaches, this problem is being addressed, making **long-term computations** possible. As Willow evolves, it will enable the creation of **AI systems** that are not just capable of performing routine tasks, but of **learning** and **adapting** in ways that are more fluid and more nuanced than anything we've seen with today's technology.

Furthermore, Willow's success is also helping to **push the boundaries of AI** in other ways. Quantum computing has the potential to **optimize complex decision-making processes** that classical AI struggles with. For example, in **healthcare**, Willow-powered AI could analyze enormous datasets of medical information and simulations to provide insights that might take years for human researchers to uncover. In **finance**, it could analyze market trends, risks, and opportunities across entire global economies in real-time, forecasting changes with a level of precision and foresight that is far beyond current capabilities. In **robotics**, Willow's power could enable machines to process information about their environments with remarkable speed and accuracy, allowing for more autonomous decision-making in real-world scenarios.

Perhaps the most exciting aspect of Willow's potential is its role in laying the groundwork for **quantum-powered AI** systems that could tackle **global challenges** in new and unprecedented ways. Problems like **climate change**, **sustainable energy**, and **disease eradication** all require multi-faceted solutions that traditional

AI and classical computing simply can't handle. With **Willow**, we are moving toward the possibility of **AI systems that can think holistically**, accounting for countless variables, and coming up with innovative solutions that were previously out of reach.

In a future where **artificial superintelligence** is powered by quantum computing, we could see machines that are not only vastly more intelligent than humans in certain areas but that can also work alongside humanity to **solve complex problems** in ways that are beyond our current understanding. Quantum AI will bring a new level of intelligence and problem-solving to industries, economies, and even everyday life, paving the way for a future where technology works in harmony with human goals.

Willow's innovations and its **quantum capabilities** are setting the stage for this future, making it a cornerstone in the **evolution of artificial superintelligence**. The journey from basic quantum computing to quantum AI and, ultimately, artificial superintelligence is just beginning, but with milestones like Willow's breakthroughs, we are closer than ever to realizing a future where quantum-powered AI is not just a dream but an integral part of our technological landscape.

Chapter 9: The Bigger Picture: How Willow Will Transform the World

As quantum computing continues to make significant strides, the ripple effect on fields like **artificial intelligence (AI)**, **machine learning**, and **data science** cannot be overstated. Willow, with its groundbreaking advancements, is poised to be the catalyst for the next monumental leap in these technologies. The impact it will have is not just incremental; it promises to **revolutionize** entire industries, redefining what's possible in computation and AI.

In AI, traditional algorithms that power everything from search engines to personalized recommendations are built on classical computing principles. These systems, although incredibly powerful, are inherently limited by the processing capabilities of binary bits. Quantum computing, on the other hand, offers the ability to process vast amounts of data in parallel using qubits, which can exist in multiple states at once. This creates the potential for AI systems that can learn, adapt, and make decisions at speeds and levels of sophistication that are simply beyond the reach of classical systems.

With Willow, the promise of **quantum-enhanced machine learning** is now closer to reality. The system's ability to rapidly process complex datasets and solve problems that would take classical systems millennia means that AI algorithms can be trained far more efficiently. For example, training models that require vast amounts of data, like deep learning models used in image recognition or natural language processing, could be dramatically accelerated. Quantum computing could enhance the way these models generalize from data, improving both the accuracy and adaptability of AI systems.

One of the most profound impacts will be felt in **data science**, where the need to analyze and derive insights from massive, often unstructured datasets is a daily challenge. In the age of big data, traditional computers struggle to perform complex analyses in a reasonable time frame. Quantum computing, with its ability to **perform parallel computations**, could analyze data in ways that were once considered impossible. Whether it's identifying hidden patterns in medical research data, optimizing supply chains in real time, or processing astronomical data to uncover the secrets of the universe, Willow's computational power will make all of this achievable—and much faster than ever before.

At the core of these advancements is **quantum machine learning (QML),** a nascent field that is poised to change the entire landscape of AI development. QML takes advantage of quantum computing's unique properties, such as **superposition** and **entanglement**, to perform tasks that classical computers simply cannot. This includes the ability to handle much more complex datasets, reduce the time required for training models, and even solve optimization problems that have stumped researchers for years. For example,

QML could be used to tackle the **traveling salesman problem** or **optimization problems in logistics** far more efficiently than classical approaches.

Beyond the realm of AI, **Willow's quantum capabilities** will undoubtedly influence the broader tech industry. With its unparalleled speed and efficiency, Willow will accelerate the development of new technologies across various sectors, from **healthcare** and **finance** to **cybersecurity** and **materials science**. In the realm of **drug discovery**, quantum computing could dramatically shorten the timeline for finding new medications by simulating molecular interactions more effectively than current systems allow. In **finance**, Willow could enable real-time risk assessments and portfolio optimizations that were once the realm of science fiction.

Even in **cybersecurity**, Willow could play a pivotal role. While there are concerns about the ability of quantum computers to crack existing encryption systems, the focus is shifting toward **quantum-safe encryption methods**—new forms of cryptography that will protect sensitive data in a quantum-powered world. Willow's advancements in **quantum error correction** and its stable architecture are critical in ensuring that the security of quantum computing is reliable and robust enough to support these innovations.

The potential of Willow in **artificial intelligence**, **machine learning**, and **data science** is not just about making existing systems faster or more efficient. It's about creating entirely new paradigms for how we think about computation. With Willow's breakthroughs, we are moving into an era where AI isn't just a tool that performs predefined tasks, but rather a system that can autonomously adapt, optimize, and innovate in ways we have yet to fully comprehend. As AI and quantum computing continue to converge, we will begin to see systems that not only mimic human intelligence but enhance it, offering solutions to problems that were once considered too complex or too time-consuming to tackle.

Quantum computing is, without a doubt, the next great frontier in technology, and Willow is at the forefront of this revolution. As we look to the future, the **synergy between quantum computing and AI** promises to transform how we solve problems, innovate, and interact with the world around us. This is just the beginning of a journey into a new technological era, and Willow is helping to lead the way, ushering in a future that was once the stuff of dreams but is now rapidly becoming our new reality.

As the rise of quantum computing becomes more tangible, its effects will reverberate far beyond the world of technology. The implications for society and the global economy are profound and multifaceted, touching everything from industry transformation to the very nature of how we work, innovate, and interact with the planet. **Willow,** with its breakthrough innovations in quantum computing, will not only catalyze change in individual sectors but will also fundamentally reshape the dynamics of entire industries and economies.

The first major shift will come in the way industries operate. **Quantum computing** promises to supercharge sectors such as **pharmaceuticals, energy, transportation, finance,** and **agriculture**. Take, for example, the field of **medicine**. With its ability to simulate complex molecular interactions far more efficiently than traditional computers, quantum systems like Willow could expedite the discovery of new drugs and treatments. Diseases that have long eluded researchers, such as certain types of cancer or Alzheimer's, could suddenly become more manageable, as quantum computing helps uncover the underlying causes and assists in the development of personalized treatment plans.

Quantum computing also holds the key to solving **complex optimization problems** that could have far-reaching implications for everything from supply chains to urban planning. By using quantum algorithms to analyze vast datasets, industries could optimize production lines, reduce waste, and increase efficiency in ways that were once impossible. **Willow's capabilities** will lead to more sustainable and efficient manufacturing, driving down costs and reducing environmental footprints. Quantum-enhanced algorithms will help industries like **logistics** and **transportation** create more effective routing systems, optimizing everything from shipping routes to the flow of traffic in urban centers.

On a larger scale, quantum computing will influence the **global economy** itself. As **businesses adopt quantum technologies**, those with access to powerful quantum systems like Willow will gain a distinct competitive advantage. Companies in fields such as **finance** will be able to process vast amounts of market data in real time, enabling them to predict market trends, assess risk more accurately, and automate trading strategies that would be impossible with classical computing methods. Financial institutions will be able to offer services that are not only faster but also more secure, thanks to quantum encryption technologies.

At the same time, however, the rise of quantum computing also presents new challenges. While the **efficiency gains** from quantum systems will drive economic growth in certain sectors, it could also disrupt existing industries and job markets. As more businesses adopt quantum technology, there will be a greater need for specialized workers skilled in quantum programming, quantum hardware, and quantum machine learning. Traditional tech jobs may be displaced, and the demand for quantum talent will only continue to grow. This creates the potential for a **skills gap**, where individuals without quantum expertise may find it increasingly difficult to keep up with the changing job landscape. Governments, industries, and educational institutions will need to collaborate to ensure that the workforce is adequately trained to meet the needs of a quantum-powered future.

In the context of **climate change**, quantum computing has the potential to be a game-changer. **Willow's speed and computational power** could drastically improve the accuracy of climate models, enabling researchers to better understand and predict the effects of global warming. Quantum simulations could also play a key role in finding **new materials** for renewable energy sources, as well as discovering ways to capture and store carbon emissions more effectively. The ability to optimize energy consumption at a granular level could make industries more sustainable, and quantum-enhanced AI could help create new solutions for everything from smart grids to energy-efficient transportation systems.

Another exciting implication lies in **engineering and material science**. Quantum computing's ability to simulate molecular and atomic structures at an unprecedented scale opens the door to a new era of innovation in **nanotechnology**, **metallurgy**, and **materials design**. New materials with properties not previously possible could revolutionize industries ranging from construction to space exploration. For example, quantum simulations could help engineers develop materials with greater strength, better conductivity, and enhanced resilience. In the **automotive** industry, quantum-enhanced simulations could lead to the creation of lighter, more fuel-efficient vehicles that use alternative materials, reducing reliance on fossil fuels and minimizing environmental impact.

Artificial intelligence will also benefit from this quantum revolution, but the impact will go beyond just AI. The integration of quantum computing into other fields will create **new hybrid technologies** that can address complex global issues. For example, AI-powered systems could be used to monitor and optimize global supply chains, ensuring that goods are distributed more equitably and efficiently. In healthcare, the fusion of AI and quantum computing could enable doctors to personalize treatments for patients based on genetic data, dramatically improving health outcomes.

While all these advancements promise significant societal and economic benefits, they also bring challenges that must be addressed. **Ethical considerations** will arise, particularly in the realm of **data privacy**, **security**, and **equity**. As quantum computing opens up new possibilities for analyzing data, concerns about how personal information is handled and who controls this data will become increasingly important. Moreover, the potential for **disruption** in certain industries means that we must carefully consider how these technologies are implemented to ensure that the benefits are distributed equitably across society.

Ultimately, the rise of **quantum computing**, driven by innovations like **Willow**, will reshape the world in ways we can only begin to imagine. It promises to solve some of humanity's most pressing problems—accelerating progress in medicine, mitigating climate change, and ushering in new breakthroughs in technology. However, it also requires careful thought about how to balance the potential for progress with the need for responsible, equitable development. As we continue to unlock the power of quantum computing, we must be mindful of the implications for society, ensuring that these advances benefit all of humanity while addressing the challenges that come with such revolutionary technology.

Conclusion

As we stand on the precipice of a new era in computing, it's impossible not to be awed by the monumental strides being made. Willow, Google's groundbreaking quantum chip, has not only redefined what we thought was possible but has also given us a glimpse into the future—a future where the boundaries of computing are no longer confined by the limitations of classical systems. In this leap, we've witnessed the convergence of decades of theoretical work and technological innovation, bringing us to a place where quantum computing is no longer a mere concept but a practical reality. Willow is the harbinger of this shift, standing as a testament to the incredible potential that lies ahead.

By breaking through traditional boundaries, Willow has demonstrated that quantum systems can achieve the unthinkable. The ability to scale quantum systems without the associated instability, the development of error-correction mechanisms that ensure reliability, and the extraordinary speed at which it operates are just the beginning of what quantum computing can accomplish. As Willow pushes the envelope, we are left to wonder what other feats it might achieve as its potential continues to unfold. With every milestone, we move closer to a world where complex problems are solved in a fraction of the time it would take today, unlocking answers to some of humanity's greatest challenges.

Yet, despite the incredible advancements represented by Willow, the journey of quantum computing is far from over. This is merely the start of a long, ongoing adventure that will see quantum technologies evolve and mature. We are still in the early stages of harnessing the full power of quantum systems, and there are many hurdles yet to overcome, from refining quantum error correction to building truly fault-tolerant quantum computers. But with the momentum behind Willow, and the relentless pursuit of quantum breakthroughs by researchers and engineers worldwide, there's no telling how far we can go.

Looking to the future, Willow—and other quantum systems like it—hold the promise of revolutionizing not just computing, but the very fabric of technology itself. From artificial intelligence and cryptography to healthcare and climate change, quantum computers will unlock new possibilities that were previously beyond our reach. The fusion of quantum computing with other fields of science will create transformative innovations that will change the way we solve problems, think about data, and interact with the world.

In the grand scheme of things, Willow is just one chapter in a much larger story. The full impact of quantum computing will unfold over decades, and its true potential will only become clearer as we continue to innovate and build upon what has already been achieved. But for now, as we look ahead, it's clear that we are on the cusp of a technological revolution unlike any we have seen before. A revolution that will reshape our world in ways we are only beginning to understand. The future of quantum computing is here, and with it comes the promise of a brighter, more efficient, and more interconnected world.

And as we move forward, one thing is certain: Willow is not just a quantum leap in technology; it's a leap for humanity itself.